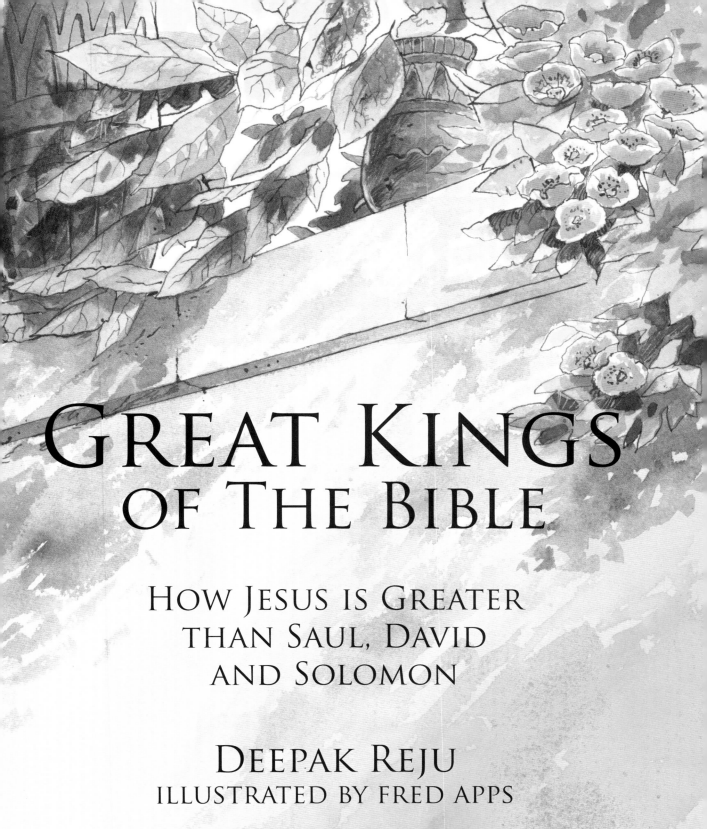

GREAT KINGS
OF THE BIBLE

HOW JESUS IS GREATER
THAN SAUL, DAVID
AND SOLOMON

DEEPAK REJU
ILLUSTRATED BY FRED APPS

CF4•K

The three greatest kings of Israel were Saul, David, and Solomon. Saul was taken from the lowly tribe of Benjamin and made the first king of Israel. David, a mere shepherd boy, led Israel's army to great victories. Solomon, one of David's many sons, was the wisest of all kings, and built a temple for God. When we look at the lives of these three kings, we see great success, but we also see failures. Their faults remind us that there is only one true King—Jesus, God's Son and our great Savior. Jesus is the greatest of all kings.

My name is King Saul, and I am the first king in Israel. This is my story ...

Give Us a King

When the prophet, Samuel, was old, he appointed his sons as judges over Israel. But his sons did not walk in his ways. They took bribes and perverted justice.

Soon afterwards, the elders came to Samuel. "You are old, and your sons do not walk in your ways. Appoint for us a king to judge us, like all the other nations."

Samuel was displeased. But the Lord said to Samuel: "Listen to the people. It is not you they are rejecting, but me as their king. Solemnly warn them what a king will do and then give them a king."

A King is Appointed

Samuel summoned the people of Israel. The Lord spoke through Samuel, "I brought you up out of Egypt and delivered you. But you have rejected me, your God who saved you. Instead you said, 'Set a king over us.'"

"So now present yourself before me by tribes and clans."

Samuel brought all of the tribes near and Benjamin was chosen. Then Matri's clan was chosen.

Then finally Saul son of Kish was chosen. But when they looked for him, they couldn't find him. So they asked the Lord, "Where is this man? Has he come here yet?"

And the Lord said, "He has hidden himself among the baggage."
They ran and brought him out, and he was taller than any
of the others. Samuel said, "Do you see the man the Lord has
chosen? There is no one like him among all of Israel."
Then the people shouted, "Long live the king!"

The New King Rescues Jabesh

Nahash the Ammonite and his armies came to attack the city of Jabesh Gilead. The people of Jabesh pleaded with Nahash, "Make a treaty with us and we will serve you."

Nahash replied, "I will make a treaty with you only if I get to gouge out the right eye of every one of you and bring disgrace on all of Israel."

Messengers from Jabesh were sent to Saul. As he was told the difficult news, the Spirit of the Lord came upon him in great power.

He burned with anger, took two oxen, and cut them into pieces. He sent them throughout Israel with a message: "This is what will be done to the oxen of anyone who does not follow Saul and Samuel to fight against the Ammonites."

A great many Israelites came out to meet Saul that day, numbering three hundred and thirty thousand.

Saul sent messengers to the people of Jabesh Gilead, "Tomorrow, by the time the sun is hot, you will be delivered from your enemies."

The very next
day, Saul's men
broke into the camp
of the Ammonites and struck
them down until midday.

Those who survived were scattered everywhere.
After this great battle, the Israelites reaffirmed Saul as their
king. Saul and all of Israel rejoiced greatly that day.

Saul Loses the Kingdom

Samuel came to Saul and once again spoke on behalf of the Lord: "I will punish the Amalekites for the way they opposed the Israelites when they came from Egypt. Destroy everyone and everything. Do not spare anything."

Saul mustered his troops and attacked the Amalekites. The Lord gave them a great victory on that day.

However, Saul and his army spared Agag, king of the Amalekites, and the best of the sheep, cattle and lambs. Anything that was weak and worthless they destroyed.

Then the word of the Lord came to Samuel: "I regret that I have made Saul king because he has disobeyed me. He did not carry out my instructions to destroy everything in Amalek."

When Samuel heard this, he was greatly troubled, and he cried out to the Lord all night long.

Early the next morning, Samuel went to Saul. He asked, "What is the bleating of sheep and lowing of the cattle that I hear?"

Saul replied: "My men spared the best of sheep and cattle to sacrifice to the Lord, but we destroyed everything else."

Samuel questioned Saul, "God told you to destroy everything. Why do you not obey the Lord?"

"But I did obey the Lord," Saul responded, "I destroyed the Amalekites. And the best sheep and cattle were saved to make sacrifices to the Lord our God."

Samuel replied, "You did not obey the Lord. You did not destroy everything in Amalek. Does the Lord delight in offerings and sacrifices more than obeying his voice? To obey is better than sacrifices. Because you rejected the word of the Lord, he has rejected you as king over Israel."

Saul realized the wrong he had done and said to Samuel: "I have sinned. I have disobeyed the Lord and not followed your instructions. I was afraid of the people, so I listened to them instead of obeying the Lord's commands. Forgive my sin and come back to worship with me."

Samuel refused Saul's request, and as he turned around, Saul caught hold of his robe and it tore.

Samuel declared: "The Lord has torn the kingdom from you and will make another man king over Israel, someone who is better than you."

Who was going to be the next king of Israel? In the days ahead, Samuel would anoint a young shepherd boy from Bethlehem named David.

Saul is Jealous of David

Saul and his army feared Goliath, the Philistine giant. No one dared to oppose him.

At his father's request, the young shepherd boy, David, came to visit his brothers on the front lines of the battle. Seeing that everyone was afraid of Goliath, David offered to fight the giant. "Let no one lose heart," David said to King Saul, "Your servant will fight this Philistine. This battle is the Lord's and he will deliver Goliath into our hands."

With a sling and a rock, David struck Goliath on the forehead, and he fell down dead.

When the men returned home from the battle with the Philistines, the women came out and met King Saul and his army. They danced and sang: "Saul has slain his thousands, and David his tens of thousands."

When Saul heard their song, he grew very angry. "They have credited him with tens of thousands, and me with only thousands. What more does he have left to gain, but to take away my kingdom?"

From that day on Saul was jealous of David. He was afraid that the people were going to love David more than him.

The next day, David was playing the harp and Saul thought, "I will pin him to the wall." Saul threw a spear at David, but David eluded him twice.

Saul lived with great fear and suspicion of David, and so he tried to kill him. For many years, Saul pursued David.

The Promise of a Greater King

Just like you and me, Saul was a sinner. He made many mistakes in his life. Saul disobeyed the word of the Lord and the instructions of the prophet Samuel.

He had a greater fear of people than for the Lord. He was jealous of David and tried many times to kill him.

Because of Saul's disobedience, fear, and jealousy, the Lord rejected Saul as king.

Many years later, God would make a promise about an even greater king who would come.

God sent his Son, Jesus, who was born in a stable. When he grew up, Jesus increased in strength and wisdom, just like we do, but he was without any sin. Jesus was different. He is a very different king.

He is not a king to be afraid of, he is loving. Jesus cared for tax collectors, sinners and many whom no one else would love.

Jesus was not jealous or suspicious, but humble. He served the sick, the poor, and the needy, and even washed his own disciples' feet.

Jesus was never disobedient, but perfectly obedient to the will of his Father. Jesus was obedient to death, even death on a cross.

Because of Jesus' death on the cross, God made him the greatest of all kings.

Death is Not the End

At the end of his life, Saul took his own life, and his body was hung on a wall by his enemies.

When the people of Jabesh Gilead heard what the Philistines had done to Saul, they came and removed his body from the wall. They burned his body and his bones were buried under a tree.

At the end of his life, Jesus was hung on a cross by his enemies.

When Joseph of Arimathea heard what had happened, he came and took down Jesus' body from the cross. Joseph wrapped it in strips of linen and placed it in a tomb.

Saul's life ended in battle, but Jesus rose again and became the greatest of all kings.

My name is King David, and
I am one of the greatest kings of Israel.
This is my story ...

David the Young Man

Young David was a shepherd, tending his father's sheep. One day the prophet Samuel came to David's home and anointed him with oil in the presence of his family. In due time, he would become the King of Israel. But until then, David showed great trust in God. With God's help, he fought and slew Goliath, the Philistine giant.

As a soldier in King Saul's army, David fought against Israel's many enemies. He had great success because the Lord was with him.

Saul was afraid of David because of his great success. Saul pursued David and tried to kill him, but David refused to take the life of the king whom God had chosen.

David Becomes King

In the course of time, King Saul and his son Jonathan died. Jonathan was killed fighting the Philistines. David grieved greatly for them. He mourned, wept, and fasted.

Soon afterward, the leaders of Judah, and then the elders of Israel, anointed David as their new king.

David and his men conquered the Jebusites and took over Jerusalem. He took up residence in the fortress and made it his capital city. It was called the City of David.

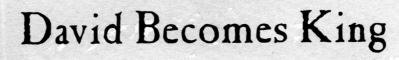

David leaped and danced before the Lord as he and the Israelites brought the Ark of the Lord to Jerusalem.

He defeated many of his enemies and subdued them because the Lord gave him victory wherever he went.

David also showed great kindness to Jonathan's son Mephibosheth, giving back his grandfather's land and inviting him to eat at the king's table for the rest of his life.

He wrote psalms of worship, praising God for the many ways the Lord preserved his life.

David and Bathsheba

At a time when kings go off to war, David sent Joab and his army to fight against the Ammonites. But David remained in Jerusalem.

One evening, when David was walking on the roof of his palace, he saw Bathsheba bathing. She was very beautiful. Although Bathsheba was not his wife, David sent messengers to fetch her. She came to him and he slept with her.

Some time later, Bathsheba sent word to David, saying, "I am pregnant."

David tried to cover up his sin. He sent for Bathsheba's husband, Uriah the Hittite, who was fighting alongside Joab and the Israelite army.

David talked with Uriah, ate with him, drank with him, and even got him drunk. David did everything he could to encourage Uriah to go home to sleep with his wife, so that it would look like the baby belonged to Uriah, not David. Yet, Uriah refused to go. He slept at the entrance of the palace instead of returning to his home.

"My duty is to the army. How can I go home to be with my wife when my commander, Joab, and the Israelite army are on the battlefield? As surely as I live, I will not do such a thing!"

David's first sin was now multiplying. Rather than confess his wrong, David sent Uriah back to the war. He wrote a letter to Joab instructing him to put Uriah where the fighting was fiercest, so he would die.

Joab followed David's instructions. When Uriah was in the most dangerous part of the battle, Joab withdrew his troops. Uriah died and King David was guilty of murder.

After Uriah's death, David took Bathsheba to be his wife. She bore him a son. But the Lord was displeased with what David had done.

So the Lord sent Nathan the prophet to speak to David. Nathan told him this story:

"There were two men, a rich man and a poor man. The rich man had many sheep and cattle, but the poor man had one ewe lamb, whom he loved and cared for—it grew up as part of his family."

"One day the rich man took away the ewe lamb from the poor man and had it prepared for his guests. He did this even though he had many sheep and cattle of his own."

David got very angry when he heard Nathan's story, "The man who did this deserves to die!"

Nathan said to David, "You are the man. You struck down Uriah the Hittite with the sword and took his wife to be your own. Because you did this, the sword will never depart from your house and the son born to you will die."

David was grieved by his sin and he responded to Nathan, "I have sinned against the Lord."

Though he pleaded with God and fasted for his child, several days later the baby died.

David Loses the Kingdom to Absalom

In due time, Nathan's prophecy was fulfilled as hatred and strife fell upon David's family.

David's son Amnon did great evil against his sister, Tamar. Their brother Absalom sought revenge and killed Amnon. Then Absalom overthrew his father, David, and took away his kingdom.

David fled across the Jordan with his army and his household. Absalom's soldiers pursued David and fought against his army. In the midst of this battle, Absalom's hair got caught in a tree. Joab found him hanging there and struck him dead. Absalom's death meant the end of the war.

David and his household returned to Jerusalem. They were greeted by many from Judah and Israel.

The Promise of a Greater King

Just like you and me, David was a sinner. He made many mistakes in his life. He was a murderer and an adulterer. He selfishly took Bathsheba to be his wife and killed her husband, Uriah. He acted unjustly when he neglected to punish Amnon for his evil against Tamar. He was conceited and full of pride when he made Joab count the number of fighting men in Israel and Judah.

David's life, which had begun with such honor and promise, was plagued with sin and disgrace. David was not the greatest king in Israel… Many years later, God made a promise about an even greater king who would come. God sent his Son, Jesus, who was born, not in a palace, but in a stable. When he grew up, Jesus increased in strength and wisdom, just like we do, but he was without any sin. Jesus was a very different kind of king than David had been. Unlike David, Jesus never killed anyone. He used his power to raise the dead to life. Jesus was never selfish, unjust, arrogant or proud.

He served the sick, the poor, and the needy. He loved those who were despised and welcomed the outcasts. He showed mercy to even the "worst" of sinners and many whom no one else would love.

He humbled himself and became obedient to death, even death on a cross!

Because of Jesus' death on the cross, God made Jesus the greatest of all kings.

Death is Not the End

When David was old, he made Solomon, Bathsheba's second son, the next king.

"Praise be to the Lord, who has allowed me to see my son Solomon become successor to my throne."

When the time drew close for David to die, he gave this charge to Solomon: "Be strong and brave. Observe what the Lord requires of you and walk in his ways."

After forty years as king, David died and was buried with his ancestors in Jerusalem.

After thirty-three years as king, Jesus died on a cross and was placed in a tomb.

David died and was buried; his life ended, but Jesus rose again and became the greatest of all kings.

My name is King Solomon, and I am the wisest king
who ever lived. This is my story ...

Solomon's Wisdom

One day, God appeared to King Solomon in a dream and said, "Ask whatever you want from me."

Solomon said, "This land has many people. Give me wisdom, so I can decide between right and wrong."

God was so pleased that Solomon asked for wisdom, and not fame and riches, that he gave him all three.

Soon afterwards, two women came to Solomon with a problem:

"This woman and I were asleep in the same house. We both had newborn babies. In the night, she rolled onto her baby and it died. So she took my baby and gave me her dead baby."

"Not true!" the other woman cried out. "The baby belongs to me. Her baby died; not mine." And so they argued in front of the king until Solomon interrupted them. "Bring me a sword," he demanded. "Cut the baby in two. Give half to this woman and half to the other."

The real mother then insisted: "Please, my king, give her the living baby. Don't kill him!"

The other said, "He shall be neither mine nor yours. Cut him in two!"

Solomon gave his ruling, "Give the living baby to the first woman. Do not kill him. She is his mother."

When the people heard Solomon's verdict, they were in awe of the king. They could see that God had given Solomon much wisdom.

A Visitor From a Far Away Land

Solomon's fame spread to many lands. The Queen of Sheba heard about his great wisdom and visited him so she could test him with hard questions.

Arriving in Jerusalem, she came with a vast caravan — camels carrying spices, large quantities of gold, and precious stones. She told Solomon all that she had on her mind. He answered all of her questions. Solomon was a very wise king.

When the Queen of Sheba saw Solomon's wisdom, the great temple and palace he had built, the food on his table, the wide array of officials, servants and cupbearers, as well as the burnt offerings he gave at the temple, she was amazed.

"The report I heard about your wisdom, wealth, and achievements is all true. I did not believe these things until I saw them with my own eyes. Praise be to God who delighted in you and made you king."

Solomon's Temple

Solomon's father was the great King David. When David was a young shepherd boy, the prophet Samuel anointed him and made him king over all of Israel.

King David and his mighty army fought many battles against his enemies. He protected the people of Israel and had many great victories.

One day, David was speaking with the prophet Nathan, "I live in a great house of cedar, and yet the ark of God only sits in a tent. I will build a temple for our great God."

That night God spoke to Nathan in a dream, and Nathan went to David. "Listen to what the Lord says, 'You will not build me a temple because you have shed so much blood. Your son will build me a temple instead of you.'"

Many years later, God's promise was fulfilled. Solomon built a magnificent golden temple for the Lord God.

The Promise of a Future King

God made another promise to Solomon's father, King David. "After you die, I will raise up one of your offspring to succeed you. He will reign on his throne forever."

Was David's son, Solomon, the everlasting king? Solomon had wisdom, riches, power, and fame. Would Solomon's reign last forever?

Just like you and me, Solomon was a sinner. Though he had great wisdom, he also lived foolishly.

He was greedy. He collected vast amounts of gold and horses.

He was proud. He spent much more time and money building his own palace, than God's temple.

He was selfish. Even though God said a man can only have one wife, Solomon married a great number of women.

He was arrogant. Even though God warned the Israelites not to take foreign wives, he took many in marriage.

He worshiped false gods. When Solomon was old, his foreign wives led him astray and convinced him to worship idols and false gods. Solomon's heart was no longer devoted to the Lord God.

Despite all of his wisdom, Solomon failed to obey the Lord God. He would not be God's everlasting king.

Who could be this promised future king?

The Everlasting King

Many years later, God sent his Son, Jesus, who was born in
a stable.

When Jesus grew up he was wise. He always had
an answer for the religious officials' hard questions. Jesus was
powerful. He healed the blind, the lame, and the sick. Jesus was
humble. He served his own disciples by washing their feet.

Jesus was mighty. Even the wind and the waves obeyed him.

Jesus was loving. He cared for tax collectors, sinners and many whom no one else would love.

Despite all of the great things he did, Jesus' greatest act was his death on the cross. He is the great Redeemer.

The child who was born in a stable became the king who gave his life on a cross so that we as sinners could be saved from the penalty of our sin if we turn from sin and trust in Christ. Jesus is a very different king indeed.

Death is Not the End

After forty years as king, Solomon died and was buried with his ancestors. After thirty-three years on this earth, Jesus died on a cross and was placed in a tomb.

When Solomon died, it was the end of Solomon's life, but three days after Jesus' death, Jesus rose again. Jesus' kingdom will go on forever. He is the everlasting king.

CHRISTIAN FOCUS PUBLICATIONS

Christian Focus · Christian Heritage · CF4K · Mentor

10 9 8 7 6 5 4 3 2 1

© Copyright 2014 Deepak Reju

ISBN 978-1-78191-291-1

Published by Christian Focus Publications, Geanies House,
Fearn, Tain, Ross-shire, IV20 1TW, Scotland, U.K.
Tel: +44 (0)1862 871011 Fax: +44 (0)1862 871699
www.christianfocus.com   email: info@christianfocus.com
Cover design by Daniel van Straaten   Illustrations by Fred Apps
Printed and bound in China

CF4·K
Because you're never
too young to know Jesus

Christian Focus Publications publishes books for adults and children under its four main imprints: Christian Focus, CF4K, Mentor and Christian Heritage. Our books reflect our conviction that God's Word is reliable and Jesus is the way to know him, and live for ever with him. Our children's publication list includes a Sunday School curriculum that covers pre-school to early teens, and puzzle and activity books. We also publish personal and family devotional titles, biographies and inspirational stories that children will love. If you are looking for quality Bible teaching for children then we have an excellent range of Bible stories and age-specific theological books. From pre-school board books to teenage apologetics,
we have it covered!
Find us at our web page: www.christianfocus.com

Deepak accurately tells the story of three great Old Testament kings. Then, he intentionally draws out the contrasts between these kings and our great King Jesus. Fred Apps' illustrations are beautiful as always and complement the comparisons. Deepak uses the phrase "Jesus is a different kind of king" as part of a paragraph refrain at the end of each section. By the end of the book, you almost want to sing out "Jesus is different. Jesus is better. Jesus is the true King."

Jared Kennedy, Family Pastor, Sojourn Community Church, Louisville, KY

In exposing the sin in the lives of Saul, David, and Solomon, Deepak Reju shows convincingly that Christ is our true hero and the greatest of all kings. While many cute Bible story books help build familiarity with the Bible in our kids' lives, we as parents need books like *Great Kings of the Bible* to help our kids see the evil of sin and stir their need for a Savior. It is then when Jesus truly becomes the Greatest King for each of them.

Marty Machowski, Pastor and Author of The Gospel Story Bible *and the* Gospel Story Curriculum

Great Kings of the Bible is an honest look at Israel's three great kings and how they point to the resurrected Christ, the true and greatest King."

Mark Smith, Pastor of Children's Ministry at Clifton Baptist Church, Louisville, KY

Deepak Reju loves Jesus and this book reflects his affections. He leads kids to see the one true and perfect King to come. A great book for any parent wanting to teach their kids how God used the imperfect kings Saul, David and Solomon to set the stage for the ultimate king, God's son - Jesus.

Jeff Hutchings, Director of Family Ministries, The Journey - St. Louis, MO

This book displays how God's covenant faithfulness to His people is carried out in the lives of Saul, David, and Solomon. What is unique and powerful is how at the end of each king's life, an aspect of King Jesus' life and saving work is highlighted. This book emphasizes that if God has determined to redeem a people for Himself, then nothing can overcome that, not even the pride, sin, and foolishness of man."

Maureen Bradley, Youth Christian Education Director, Christ Presbyterian Church, Richmond, IN

Deepak does a great job of helping children understand the history of the kings of old – in both their triumphs and failures. But more than that, he directs their attention toward Jesus, the great and promised king who walked in perfect wisdom, humility and righteousness in a way no earthly king ever could. This book will serve as a helpful resource in the quest to show children how the Old Testament continually points to Jesus.

Anne Lincoln Holibaugh, Children's Minister, The Village Church, Flower Mound, TX